Someone Very Important
Has Just Died

also by Mary Turner

**Talking with Children and Young People
about Death and Dying
A Workbook**
Mary Turner
Illustrated by Bob Thomas
ISBN 1 85302 563 1

of related interest

**Children, Bereavement and Trauma
Nurturing Resilience**
Paul Barnard, Ian Morland and Julie Nagy
ISBN 1 85302 785 5

Interventions with Bereaved Children
Susan C. Smith and Sister Margaret Pennells
ISBN 1 85302 285 3

**Helping Children to Manage Loss
Positive Strategies for Renewal and Growth**
Brenda Mallon
ISBN 1 85302 605 0

**The Forgotten Mourners, Second Edition
Guidelines for Working with Bereaved Children**
Susan C. Smith
ISBN 1 85302 758 8

The Inspiration of Hope in Bereavement Counselling
John R. Cutcliffe
Foreword by Ronna Jevne
ISBN 1 84310 082 7

**Grief in Children
A Handbook for Adults**
Atle Dyregrov
ISBN 1 85302 113 X

Someone Very Important Has Just Died

Immediate Help for People Caring
for Children of All Ages at the Time
of a Close Bereavement

Mary Turner

Illustrated by Elaine Bailey

Jessica Kingsley Publishers
London and Philadelphia

First published in 2005
by Jessica Kingsley Publishers
116 Pentonville Road
London N1 9JB, UK
and
400 Market Street, Suite 400
Philadelphia, PA 19106, USA

www.jkp.com

Library of Congress Cataloging in Publication Data
Turner, Mary, 1949-
Someone very important has just died : immediate help for people caring for children of all ages at the time of a close bereavement / Mary Turner ; illustrated by Elaine Bailey.
p. cm.
Includes bibliographical references.
ISBN 1-84310-295-1 (pbk.)
1. Bereavement in children. 2. Children and death. 3. Child rearing. I. Title.
BF723.G75T87 2004
155.9'37'083—dc22

2004012507

British Library Cataloguing in Publication Data
A CIP catalogue record for this book is available from the British Library

ISBN-13: 978 1 84310 295 3
ISBN-10: 1 84310 295 1

Printed and Bound in Great Britain by
Athenaeum Press, Gateshead, Tyne and Wear

With heartfelt thanks to Elizabeth

Contents

Why the need for this book?

I was recently asked to help a family in which a young wife and mother died very suddenly and unexpectedly, leaving a traumatised husband, two very little children, and a wider family of grown-ups. They were so shocked and distressed that they found it very hard to begin to even think about how to cope with the implications of the immediate situation, let alone consider how best to help the children. Particular problems in this respect were how to tend to the children, what to say to them, how far to include them in the immediate events following the death, and in what ways.

I found myself writing notes and suggestions on pieces of paper as to what the adults might do and say, because of course they were all finding it impossible to remember what was said to them. These pieces of paper seemed important for the family. They felt they had some simple words of advice that could be followed if it seemed appropriate, and which gave them something practical to steer by in that time of crisis.

The notes and suggestions have been gathered into this small book which is designed to address the needs of people of all ages, and can be adapted to be suitable for anyone regardless of their background and beliefs. The material is as simple as possible in order to avoid overload at a time when people have a lot to think about already.

Introduction

This is written for you who have recently been bereaved, and who have children of any age, or teenagers, to care for. The book is specifically designed to help you address the needs of these children and teenagers. Any funeral director or minister or registrar of births and deaths will help you with the practical details regarding general procedures that are necessary at this time.

You are trying to cope with the events of the last few days or weeks, and you are also trying to cope with needs of the children. It is likely that there will only be a few days for plans to be made about the funeral, and perhaps you will find some of the suggestions here helpful. This book will try to keep things as brief as possible; you will have so much else on your mind that simplicity here is all important. Each section will therefore have a few main summary points.

You may be full of questions or you may be quite numb. Either way, these pages may be something of a guide for you now and in the coming weeks. You cannot be expected to remember what people say to you at the moment, which is why this book has been written. It is hoped that you will find help and support here, whatever your background and your beliefs might be.

- Show this book to someone else, perhaps a friend or relative or professional. They will be able to help you consider the points raised in it. You need the love and support of other people, be they friends, relatives or professionals, in order to help with the pain of a close bereavement.

- Remember that a newly bereaved person is going to find it very difficult to absorb too much information at any one time, and may be having trouble thinking straight. This is only to be expected.

- The needs of the children and teenagers must be considered at this time. They need care and attention from understanding and supportive adults who will not leave them out, but will draw them into what is happening in a way that they can understand and bear.

- There are addresses and phone numbers of support organisations at the end of this book where you can obtain appropriate and effective ongoing help.

1

How you may react to the death of someone close

When someone close to us dies, it is often a tremendous shock. This shock may be even more difficult to cope with if the death was unexpected. Sometimes we can be traumatised by events. Even when you know someone is about to die, it is impossible to plan for how you will react when it happens, both immediately afterwards and in the weeks to come.

Shock and grief affect how we think, and how we behave. They affect how we feel emotionally and also physically. It can be hard to concentrate and to remember things. Eating and sleeping patterns may change. We can feel numb and switched off. We may want to stay in bed to withdraw from others, or feel quite the opposite and want company all the time. We can become unwell. Thoughts and feelings can change rapidly and it can seem like being on a roller-coaster that is out of control – one moment going one way and the next another. With time, these feelings will ease, but some of them may well be problems at the moment.

- Shock and grief affect people of all ages in many different ways. Try not to let your pain and distress separate you too much from those around you. You need the support of others.

- Remember that these feelings will ease with time, and are normal. It is better to know these things than to be surprised by them. Understanding can help you to be patient with yourself and others, and can help you to believe that you will all somehow go forwards.

- See Chapter 7 *Looking after everyone's health and easing stress* for practical suggestions on helping with shock and grief.

2

How children and teenagers may react at the time of bereavement

We would like to believe that children and young people are not affected in the way that adults are by a close bereavement. We do not want to think of them hurting in any way and therefore sometimes try to convince ourselves that they are all right. Sadly however, we need to understand that even tiny babies will be affected by a close bereavement. We need to give help to everyone, whatever their age.

Babies and little children cannot use words and may therefore show their distress by changes in their behaviour, or by becoming poorly. Little children who have learned to talk will still find it very hard or even impossible to understand what has happened, and may be shocked and confused. Children and teenagers are likely to have many questions, worries, and feelings that they need help with. If they are left out of what is happening, both practically and emotionally, this will only increase their confusion and distress and may build up difficulties later. Suggestions as to how to include children at this time are made in the following sections.

Children of any age may begin to behave in the same way that they did when they were much younger. For example, they may cry more or become very clingy or return to wetting the bed. They may become more withdrawn or they may become angry. They may try to be as good and helpful as possible. As with adults, there are many ways in which children's behaviour might change.

Little children may play for a while before remembering their distress. Some children and teenagers seem to carry on regardless; they may be trying to hide their sadness in order to protect themselves or you. Children and teenagers can be puzzled and confused by all the emotions at this time.

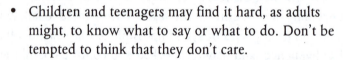

- Changes in the behaviour of children of any age is understandable and indicates that the child needs support.

- Children and teenagers may find it hard, as adults might, to know what to say or what to do. Don't be tempted to think that they don't care.

- Changes in children will pass in due course as long as they receive the support they need in the coming weeks and months. For now, the important thing is to understand that these reactions are not unusual, and that you should not expect yourself or the children to soldier on without help.

- Hugs are good and need no words. Tell the children that hugging each other helps us to feel better.

- Tell the children that grown-ups cry and become upset just like them when things are bad, but they will get better. We all have to let the tears come out before we can let go of the pain inside.

- If the children are old enough, explain that the way they are feeling is called grief and that it is truly terrible, but it is normal and will become more bearable. Being given facts like this can be very reassuring. Remember that grief is probably a new experience for a child, and therefore all the more overwhelming.

3

Getting support for yourself and the children

You will find contact telephone numbers to help you to access your nearest support services at the end of this book. Teachers, ministers, the funeral director, your GP or other members of the community should be able to offer you support and advice. Your local hospice may be able to tell you about ministers

Sorry to hear of your sad loss, please let me know if I can be of any help to you.

and funeral directors who are experienced in including the needs of children in funeral arrangements. Another very useful source of help at this time might be your local children's bereavement support service (see the *Useful contacts* section at the end of the book).

- People want to help you. Let them – providing they do not take everything out of your hands. It is important that you feel in control. Now is not the time to feel guilty or feeble about accepting or requesting help: it simply makes sense so that you and the children get through the days and weeks to come as best you can.

- Whatever the age of the children you care for, they will feel easier if they know that you are being helped both practically and emotionally by other adults. It is enormously important for your children to see that you are not having to manage all by yourself; if they can worry just a little less about you, their overall worries will be lessened.

- Include the children. Children of all ages need to be included in the plans for what happens next. Although it may seem best to leave the children out of any plans that are being made, this can create difficulties later on, when they may feel they were excluded and that their needs were not important. Practical suggestions for how you might do this follow below.

- Consider whether to keep the children out of school for a little while. If they are old enough, discuss this with them.

- Tell other people, for example teachers at school, what has happened. Ask someone else to do this for you if necessary. Do make sure that the children's college, school or playgroup know about their bereavement. It can be very helpful to talk to a teacher that you know and trust. The school will then be able to keep an eye on how the children are, and be mindful that if their performance or behaviour changes, there are reasons which may account for these changes. It can also be good to know that the school or college is watching out for the child's needs at this time. If you cannot talk to a teacher yourself, perhaps you could think of someone you could ask to do this on your behalf.

- Talk to the children before liaising with other people about them. They may want to know what you are planning to say, or they may have some ideas of their own about what they would like said, and to whom. Even quite little children can be consulted about how they would like their teacher to be told, and asked if they think there is anything that their teacher might be able to do to help. Who would be the best person to talk to the teacher, and does the child want to be present or not?

- Make a list or a drawing of all the people who love and support the children, or who are their friends. Pin it up where the children will see it and be able to get reassurance from looking at it. Tell the children that these people will help and care for them. It is nice to draw all these people in a circle with the children in the middle. Try to show the drawing to some of these people. The children may want to do this themselves, or they may want someone to help them.

4

Talking to children and young people about death and funerals

It is very hard to talk to children and young people about death and funerals. We wish to do everything we can to spare them more hurt. However, they are very likely to have lots of thoughts, questions, ideas, fears and worries that are better aired. Sometimes the thoughts and images that children and teenagers have about death have been affected by frightening television programmes, films and computer games. It is therefore important to help them realise that death can be still and peaceful rather than terrifying.

- Reassure the children that it is ok to talk about how they are feeling and about the person who has died. Explain that it is not their fault if everyone starts crying when these things are talked about. Crying lets the tears out and this can somehow make the pain inside feel a little easier. It can be good to cry even though it seems so sad to do so.

- Don't distance yourself from the children when you or they are upset. If it gets too much to bear, just say that you need a few minutes alone. Help them to do the same if they need to.

- Try to decide what you are going to say so that the children are not confused with different explanations.

5

Words you could use

Given below are some words you may find useful. Exactly what you choose to say will depend on your own situation. Read this section through and consider which points are useful to you and your circumstances.

Discuss this with the minister or funeral director or other supportive people, so that you can choose words most suited to your situation.

Try to keep what you say as simple as possible. How much to tell a child is not an easy decision to make. The best course of action is to be honest without overloading them with too much detail. Perhaps as you read these words you will find your own way forward about what to say. Perhaps other people can help you with this too.

> When people die they stop breathing and they stop thinking. Their hearts stop beating and they do not feel anything. When people die, the special part we call 'life' leaves the body. Some people call the special power of life the 'soul' or the 'spirit'. We do not know exactly what happens to this special part of people because it cannot come back to earth as a person to tell us. It does not ever come back to the body. Not ever. The body is very quiet and peaceful and still. Forever.

> Sometimes children think that it was somehow their fault that the person died, or that they should have

done something different to stop it from happening. You don't need to be thinking this.

After a person has died, the body isn't needed anymore. There is no pain and no feelings, so it is quite all right for the body to be peaceful like this. The person no longer lives in the body after they have died.

A dead person cannot come back to life again. Death is not like sleep. Dying is not like sleeping. Sleeping is part of living and helps us to grow and to feel stronger when we wake up each day.

Sometimes people's bodies are too old or too hurt or too ill to get better, however hard the doctors and nurses try.

After someone has died we can sometimes see the dead body so that we can say goodbye to it. If you would like to do that, there will be people to help you. The body will be very still and feel very different. It will also feel cold. Remember that the person who has died doesn't need the body anymore and is not feeling anything or thinking anything.

After someone has died, their friends and family come together for a special meeting. This meeting is sometimes called a funeral. At this special meeting the family and friends say goodbye to the body that is not needed anymore, and they think about the special power of life that has left the body.

Before the funeral, the dead body is put inside a coffin. A coffin is a special wooden box. The coffin has a lid. Sometimes we leave tokens such as drawings or mementos inside the coffin with the dead body. This can help us to say goodbye.

At the end of the funeral, the dead body is taken in the coffin to be buried. The coffin will be very gently lowered into a deep hole in the ground called a grave. The coffin is usually buried near a church or in another special place where bodies are buried, called a cemetery or graveyard.

Sometimes the special meeting to say goodbye to the body is at a place called a crematorium. Sometimes people choose to bury the ashes of the body and it is at a crematorium that the dead body is turned into ashes. Remember that the body feels nothing at all. Ashes are full of goodness and help the earth to be a good place for plants to grow and for life to go on in other ways.

You may have lots of questions to ask and that is fine. We will try to help you to find answers as best we can. We will look after you all the time and remember how hard everything is for you.

These words have been adapted from the book *Talking with Children and Young People about Death and Dying: A Workbook*, by Mary Turner, also published by Jessica Kingsley Publishers.

6

Immediate matters to consider regarding the funeral

The suggestions in this section need to be adapted to your particular circumstances. It is important that you consider them and discuss what to do with friends, family or professionals.

- Meet the funeral director and meet the minister. Tell them about the children, ask them how involved the children could be, and discuss the points below. They may have other ideas too. Ask if they will help you.

- Discuss whether the children should see the body and attend the funeral. If you decide that they shouldn't, then discuss alternatives, such as having time together with the children later and remembering the person who has died in a way that is special for the children. Seeing the dead body can be a very important part of helping children and teenagers to understand what has happened.

- If the children are old enough, make sure that they are consulted regarding what they would prefer to do. Make sure that the choice about whether to see the body or not is a real choice, and that if the children wish to do this, they are given proper support (see the following paragraphs). Of course it is important to respect the children's choice, and let them know that they can change their minds at any time. If they do not want to see the body, that is entirely appropriate too.

If the children do wish to see the body, talk to the funeral director or the minister about this and ask if he will help you. The children need to be told that the body is dead, and will look and feel different. It is sometimes possible to dress the body in clothes that the family choose, and you and the children may be able to leave small tokens in the coffin, such as drawings or mementos.

Even very little children can be taken to the chapel of rest to be included in what is happening. If the children do not go in to see the dead body, they can nevertheless be part of the group who have visited and can be cared for by a friend or relative whilst others are seeing the body. In this way, even the tiniest child, once he or she is older, will be able to look back and know that they were included.

The children will need to be prepared for what they will see when they go into the room where the coffin is. Usually a few brief words to explain about the coffin and what the body will look and feel like is sufficient – just enough information to enable the children to be a little prepared in their minds. This may mean that you go in first for a moment or two and then fetch the children. The children could take something with them to leave in the coffin, perhaps a drawing or some flowers.

In the same way, try to include the children in the funeral service preparation and the plans for what type of gathering may take place afterwards. They may wish to take part in some way, perhaps by helping to prepare for guests or by reading during the service. Even little children can contribute in their own way. It is helpful to explain in simple words what the children should expect at a funeral.

It may help you to identify someone to support the children at the funeral and afterwards. If you have the support of someone less emotionally involved, he or she will be able to watch out for the children at all times in case you are preoccupied with your own feelings or with practical matters.

7

Looking after everyone's health and easing stress

Shock, grief, tiredness and trauma affect us physically and emotionally, however old we are. It is very important to give the mind and body help in order to stay as steady as possible. If you are worried about any symptoms, or feel very low or desperate, your doctor is there to help. Here are some additional suggestions that others have found effective for sleeplessness and general symptoms of stress.

- Drinking plenty of pure water helps the system to function as well as possible.

- Taking nutritional supplements can support the body in times of stress.

- Herbal and homeopathic remedies are especially to be recommended for young children and babies for whom medication is not usually advised.

- Bach flower remedies are also useful.

- There are several different kinds of massage that are very soothing and should be considered for little babies and upwards.

- Try lavender oil sprinkled in bath water or onto a pillow, or used (carefully) in a burner. Do not put it directly onto the skin. It is calming and helps with sleep.

- Acupuncture can be very helpful but is not generally used with younger children.

Because little children cannot use words to express their feelings, they may express their distress through becoming poorly or by behaving in a different way. Therefore it can be useful to find a suitable support for them as outlined above.

Older children may accept one of the forms of support discussed earlier. Tell them it is only sensible to look after ourselves – just as we would do if we had a broken leg.

If you are buying any of the products suggested above, do take advice from a qualified practitioner or from the pharmacist in the shop – they may have some more suggestions too. They will need to know if the person for whom you are getting the remedy is taking any medication. You may find that friends can recommend where to go.

8

The way forward

There is such a lot to cope with in the weeks immediately following a death and a funeral. These are early days and all of the things that you put in place now for your own ongoing support and for that of the children, will be very worthwhile.

- Keep in touch with your support people. As time goes by you may want to build in some more support for yourself and the children. You may know that you need ongoing help straight away, or you may decide to review things in a few months' time. Remember that children are reassured when they know that the adults who are looking after them have help available. The help you need may be practical or emotional.

- There are many useful publications to help you to understand your own grief and the grief of the children. There are also books for children and teenagers to read themselves or have read to them. New books are constantly being published and the organisations in the *Useful contacts* section can give you guidance as to what might be suitable for you.

- Expressing grief openly is not a sign of weakness and can show children and teenagers that it is ok for them to do the same. Remember that children will be able to bear seeing your distress and sadness if they are helped to understand that this is only to be expected and that you will all start to feel better eventually.

- Get help for yourself if you continue to sleep badly, or to have intrusive images or memories of what happened, or find yourself increasingly irritable or not wanting to go on with life. Counsellors or psychotherapists trained in bereavement and trauma work will be able to help alleviate such symptoms. Get help if relationships in the family become increasingly strained. Don't hesitate to contact your GP, or any of the organisations listed in the next section – they are there to help.

- Get help for the children if you think that they are struggling in any way and you feel you need some extra advice on how they are managing. If you sense that the children have changed in some way, or are unwell, then they may be struggling to cope with their feelings and thoughts relating to the person who has died, and the effect that this death has had on them.

- Remember that all these reactions are normal and understandable.

- Be patient with yourself and with the children as the days and weeks go by. These things take time. Try to look after yourself and to find a little time away from sad things. It is important for everyone to know that somehow life can go on and that it is ok to enjoy yourself.

- Try not to feel guilty if some happiness finds its way into your life. The people who have put this book together hope it does, and wish you well.

For you and the children

In the darkness there is a star,
or a light, or a candle, or the moon.
In the shadow the sun is never far away.
In the dark earth are the seeds of spring.
In our fears and worries lie
also our strength to overcome them.
In our sadness and tears there can
also be smiles and laughter.
In our being lonely and lost,
there can be hope,
and people to comfort us.

Useful contacts

The Childhood Bereavement Network (CBN)
8 Wakley Street
London EC1V 4ET
Tel: 0207 843 6309
Email: cbn@ncb.org.uk

The CBN will provide you with the name of an organisation or an individual near you who can help with issues relating to grief and bereavement in children and teenagers.

The Child Bereavement Trust (CBT)
Aston House
High Street
West Wycombe
Bucks HP14 3AG
Tel: 01494 446648
Website: www.childbereavement.org.uk

The CBT can provide books and information and also has a website forum for bereaved families.

Hospice Information
Hospice House
34–44 Britannia Street
London WC1X 9JG
Tel: 0870 903 3903
Website: www.hospiceinformation.info

Staff at your local hospice may be able to put you in touch with appropriate people in your community who can help.

The British Association for Counselling and Psychotherapy (BACP)

1 Regent Place
Rugby
Warwickshire CV21 2PJ
Tel: 0870 443 5218
Website: www.BACP.co.uk

The BACP has a directory of counsellors who are experienced in bereavement and in trauma.

Cruse Bereavement Care

Cruse House
126 Sheen Road
Richmond
Surrey TW9 1UR
Tel: 0208 939 9530
Website: www.crusebereavementcare.org.uk

Cruse is a national bereavement support service provided by trained volunteers.

Survivors of Bereavement by Suicide (SOBS)

Centre 88
Saner Street
Hull HU3 2TR
Tel: 0870 241 3337
Website: www.uk-sobs.org.uk

SOBS is a national support service run by survivors, for survivors.